THE SECRET GARDEN

RETOLD BY PAULINE FRANCIS

EVANS BROTHERS LIMITED

Published by Evans Brothers Limited
2A Portman Mansions
Chiltern Street
London W1U 6NR

Reprinted 2007

Printed in China by WKT Company Limited

British Library Cataloguing in Publication data
Francis, Pauline
       The secret garden
       1. Gardens – Juvenile fiction 2. Yorkshire (England) –
       Juvenile fiction 3. Children's stories
       I. Title II. Burnett, Frances Hodgson, 1849 – 1924

ISBN 978 023752535 4

THE SECRET GARDEN

Introduction

Frances Hodgson Burnett was born in Manchester, a large city in the north of England, in 1849. A few years after her father's death, her family moved to America. The family was very poor, so Frances began to write stories for a magazine to earn some money. They were accepted almost straight away. In 1873, Frances married Swan Burnett.

At first, Frances Burnett wrote novels for adults. Then, as her two sons were growing up, she wrote a magazine serial for boys called *Little Lord Fauntleroy*. This was later published as a book. Other books followed: *Sara Crewe* and *The Little Princess*.

In 1909, Frances Burnett began to plant a garden at the new house she was having built in America. This gave her the idea for *The Secret Garden*. It was published in 1911 and became her best-known children's book.

The Secret Garden tells the story of an orphan, Mary Lennox, who is sent from India to live with her uncle in his big house on the Yorkshire Moors. She is a sad, sour and lonely child – as is the cousin she discovers living in the house. Through their hard work on a secret garden, both children grow strong and happy.

Frances Hodgson Burnett died in 1923.

CHAPTER ONE
Alone

Mary Lennox was a very unpleasant child. Everybody said so. She had a little thin face and a little thin body, thin fine hair and a sour expression on her face. But this was not all Mary's fault.

She was born in India, where her father was working at the time. Her mother was a great beauty who liked to have fun at parties. She did not want a little girl, and so she left the servants to look after poor Mary. Mary grew into a bad-tempered and difficult child who always wanted her own way.

One morning, when Mary was nine years old, she woke up feeling very cross. She was even more cross when she saw that her ayah – nurse – had not come to get her up.

"There is something strange going on," Mary thought, "but I do not understand what it is."

During the whole of that day, and the next, everybody seemed to have forgotten Mary. She only knew that people were ill and that the house was full of frightening noises. She hid in the nursery and nobody came to look after her. Once, she crept into the dining room and found it empty, although there was a half-eaten meal on the table. As she was thirsty, Mary drank a glass of wine. She did not know how strong it was and so she went back to the nursery and slept for a very long time.

When Mary woke up, the house was completely silent. Suddenly, she heard the sound of footsteps. A few minutes later, the door of the nursery opened. A man came in and looked very startled to see Mary.

"There is a child here!" he called to another man behind him. "Who is she?"

"I am Mary Lennox," Mary told him crossly. "Why has nobody come to look after me?"

The other man came into the room. "She has been forgotten!" he said.

"Why was I forgotten?" Mary asked, stamping her foot.

"Poor little child," the man whispered sadly. "There is nobody left to come to you. Your ayah, your parents, the servants – they have all died of cholera."

A week later, Mary was put on to a ship sailing for England. She was going to live with her uncle, Mr Archibald Craven, at Misselthwaite Manor in Yorkshire. Mr Craven's housekeeper, Mrs Medlock, came to meet Mary in London. She was a plump woman, with red cheeks and sharp black eyes. Mary did not like her at all – but then she hardly ever liked anybody. Mrs Medlock did not think much of Mary either.

"My word! She's a plain girl!" she said to herself, "and they say her mother was such a beauty. There'll be little to improve her at Misselthwaite Manor."

Mary was very curious about her uncle. What would he be like? Somebody in India had told her he was a hunchback! What was that? She began to feel lonely. Why did she never seem to belong to anybody, even when her mother and father were alive? Why did nobody take any notice of her? Of course, Mary did not know the reason – that she was an unpleasant child.

The next day, Mrs Medlock and Mary set off by train for Yorkshire. Mary had nothing to read, and she folded her thin little black-gloved hands in her lap. Her black dress made her yellow skin look even more yellow and her limp hair straggled from under her black hat.

"Do you know anything about your uncle?" Mrs Medlock asked.

"No," Mary replied.

"I may as well tell you," Mrs Medlock said, "you are going to a strange place."

Mary did not answer.

"It's a rather grand house, in a gloomy sort of way," the housekeeper carried on. "It is six hundred years old, and it's on the edge of a moor. There are hundreds of rooms, though most of them's shut up and locked. There's gardens and trees. But there's nothing else."

Mary began to listen. It all sounded so unlike India, and anything new interested her. But she did not want to look interested. That was one of the unpleasant things about her. So she sat still.

"Well," Mrs Medlock said. "What do you think of it?"

"Nothing," she replied.

"Don't you care?" Mrs Medlock asked.

"It doesn't matter whether I care or not," Mary said.

"He's got a crooked back, your uncle," Mrs Medlock said. "He was a sour young man until he married. Your aunt was such a sweet, pretty thing. When she died... Well, it made him stranger than ever. He cares about nobody. He won't see people. Most of the time he shuts himself up in his study."

None of this made Mary feel cheerful. She stared out of the window, her lips pinched together.

"There's nothing to do there," Mrs Medlock said. "You'll have to play by yourself."

A carriage met them at the railway station. When they had passed through many villages, the horses began to go more slowly, as if they were climbing uphill. Mary could see nothing except the yellow light of the carriage. The wind whistled past them in the darkness.

"I don't like it," Mary thought. "I don't like it."

And she pinched her thin lips together even more tightly.

CHAPTER TWO

A cry in the night

When Mary opened her eyes in the morning, it was because a young housemaid had come into her bedroom to light a fire. Mary lay and watched her. She had never been in such a gloomy room. Through the window, she caught sight of a stretch of land. It had no trees and looked as endless as the sea.

"What is out there?" she asked.

"That's the moor," the housemaid told her. "Does tha like it?"

"What do you mean?" Mary asked. "I don't understand your language."

"I talk too much Yorkshire," the girl laughed. "Do you like it?"

"No," Mary answered. "I hate it."

"That's because tha's not used to it," the girl said. "My name's Martha."

"Are you going to be my servant?" Mary asked.

"I'm Mrs Medlock's servant," Martha said firmly. "But I have to do the housemaid's work for you."

"Who is going to dress me?" Mary demanded.

Martha stared in amazement. "Can't tha put on tha…your own clothes?" she asked.

"No," Mary said. "My ayah always dressed me."

"Well," Martha said, "it's time tha should learn."

When she was angry, Mary had always slapped her ayah's face. She wondered what this girl would do if she slapped her face. Suddenly, Mary felt horribly lonely. She threw herself face down on the pillows and began to sob. Good-hearted Martha went over to the bed.

"Don't cry, miss," she said. "I'll help with tha clothes."

Martha talked as she helped Mary to dress – about her mother, Mrs Sowerby, and her brothers and sisters, and especially about Dickon, one of the brothers.

"He's only twelve but he's got his own pony," Martha said, "and he knows every bird and animal on the moor."

After a breakfast of porridge, which she did not enjoy, Mary glanced around her. Mrs Medlock was right. There was nothing to do.

"I am going into the garden," she told Martha. "Who will go with me?"

"Tha'll go by tha'self," Martha laughed.

She found a coat and boots and gloves for Mary and showed her the way downstairs. "One of the gardens is locked up," she told Mary. "So don't try to get in."

"Why?" Mary asked, in spite of herself.

"Mr Craven had it locked when his wife died ten years ago. It was her garden," Martha said. "Then he threw away the key."

Mary walked across wide lawns until she came to the kitchen gardens, surrounded by walls. She opened a green door in one of the walls and found herself in an orchard, full of bare fruit trees. Beyond the orchard was another wall, but no door. The tops of trees showed above the wall. When Mary stood still, she saw a bird with a bright red breast sitting on one of the branches. Suddenly, he started to sing. The sound almost brought a smile to Mary's sour little face.

Mary went back to the first of the kitchen gardens and found an old man digging there. He took no notice of her, so at last she spoke to him. "There's no door to the garden up there," she said. "I saw a bird with a red breast sitting in one of the trees. He sang to me."

To her surprise, a slow smile spread over the man's face. The old man turned his head and made a low, soft whistle. Almost the next moment, Mary heard a soft rushing through the air. It was the bird with the red breast. It settled on the ground next to the gardener.

"Will he always come when you call him?" Mary whispered.

"Aye, he will," the gardener said. "He's a robin redbreast, the friendliest bird there is. He lives over in that garden behind the wall. I think he's lonely."

"I'm lonely, too," she said. "I have no friends at all. I never had." She had not known until then that this was

one of the things that made her sour and cross.

"Then tha's like me," the gardener said. "We're both as sour as we look."

Mary went outside every day after that. The fresh winds from the moor began to blow the cobwebs out of her brain. When she sat down to eat in the evening, she felt hungry. She even got used to the sound of the wind roaring and rushing around the house.

One night, as Mary sat with Martha, she heard a strange sound. "Can you hear a child crying?" she asked.

"No," Martha replied, worried. "It's just the wind."

"But listen." Mary said. "It's in the house –" And at that very moment, the wind forced open the door, blowing out the candle. The crying filled the room.

"There!" Mary cried. "I told you! It is someone crying – and it isn't a grown-up!"

CHAPTER THREE
The secret garden

It rained for the next two days. Then the clouds slowly disappeared. Mary had never seen such a blue sky. In India, the skies were hot and blazing. This was a deep, cool blue that seemed to sparkle like the waters of a lake.

Martha had the day off to visit her family. Mary was lonely without her so she went out into the garden. The sunshine made the whole place look different. The high, deep blue sky arched over Misselthwaite Manor, as well as over the moor. The change in the weather had done the gardener, Ben Weatherstaff, good as well. He spoke to her first.

"Spring's coming," he said. "Can tha smell it?"

Mary sniffed the air. "I can smell something nice and fresh and damp," she said.

"That's good rich earth," he said, digging away. "There'll be crocuses an' snowdrops an' daffydillys pushing through soon."

The robin flew down and hopped close to Mary's feet and looked at her slyly.

"He wants to be tha friend," Ben told her.

Mary walked on, thinking hard. She had begun to like the garden just as she had begun to like the robin and

Martha – and Dickon and their mother, although she had not met them yet. That seemed a good many people to like when you were not used to liking anyone at all.

She stopped outside the wall of the locked garden. She heard the robin chirping and twittering on the edge of a hole where he was looking for worms. Mary stared into the earth. Something was buried there, something made of brass. She bent down to look. It was an old key.

"Perhaps it has been buried for ten years," she said in a whisper as she picked it up. "Perhaps it is the key to the garden! I shall look for the door."

But she could not find it. However closely she looked, she could only see thick ivy growing all over the wall. At last she put the key in her pocket and went indoors. Martha was back and had brought a present for Mary. It was a strong, thin rope with a striped red and blue handle at each end. Mary stared at it in amazement.

"What is it for?" she asked.

"For?" Martha asked. "Tha's never seen a skipping rope? Just watch me!"

She ran into the middle of the room, and taking a handle in each hand, began to skip and skip. Then she gave the skipping rope to Mary.

"Mother says you mun… you must practise first, until you get some strength into your arms and legs," she said.

Mary put on her coat and hat and turned to go.

Suddenly, she thought of something. "Martha," she said, "you spent some of your wages on me. Thank you."

Mary skipped around the garden, resting every few minutes. The robin followed her everywhere. Every time she jumped, she felt the weight of the key in her pocket.

"You showed me where the key was," Mary called out to the robin. "Now show me the door to the garden!

Mary Lennox always said what happened next was magic. As she spoke, a gust of wind blew the trailing ivy on the wall of the secret garden. Mary caught sight of the handle of a door. She drew out the key from her pocket and found that it fitted the keyhole. She turned the key. Then she pushed open the door slowly.

Now she was standing inside the secret garden.

CHAPTER FOUR
Mary meets Dickon

The garden was the most mysterious place Mary had ever seen. The high walls around it were covered with leafless roses. The ground was covered with clumps of rose bushes. There were other trees covered with climbing roses.

"How still it is!" she whispered. She watched the robin fly into his treetop. "I am the first person who has spoken here for ten years," she whispered again.

Mary did not know if the garden was dead or alive. If she had been Ben Weatherstaff, she would have known that the roses were just resting for the winter. She walked slowly through the garden. Then she stopped. "There's something sticking out of the black earth!" she whispered. "Perhaps these are the crocuses and snowdrops and daffodils Mr Weatherstaff was talking about. Even if the other plants are dead, these are alive."

Mary found a stick and dug some of the earth around the green shoots. "Now they look as if they can breathe," she told the robin.

After dinner that evening, Mary went to her seat by the fire. "Martha," she began, "I wish I had a spade."

"Whatever for, Miss Mary?" Martha asked, laughing.

"This is such a lonely place," Mary replied. "There is nobody to talk to except you and Ben Weatherstaff. I thought if I had a little spade, I could dig somewhere. I might make a little garden if I can get some seeds."

Martha's face lit up. "Dickon often goes to Thwaite village," she said. "He can get whatever you need."

"I have a shilling a week to spend," Mary said. "Will you ask him?"

"I'll send him a note," Martha said. "He'll bring them to you."

The sun shone down for nearly a week on the secret garden. Mary was beginning to like being outside. She even liked the wind. She could run faster and longer and skip up to a hundred. She worked hard in the garden, pulling up weeds and digging. Sometimes she stopped to gaze around.

"What will it be like when it is covered with thousands of flowers?" she asked herself.

During the week of sunshine, Mary got to know Ben Weatherstaff better. She was more polite to him than she used to be. He did not talk very much but one morning, he said. "Tha's fatter than tha was, and not so yellow."

"I know," she replied, "my stockings are tighter. Mr Weatherstaff, if you had a garden of your own, a flower garden, what would you plant?"

"Mostly roses," he said. "I used to be the gardener to the master's wife. She loved roses. I've seen her bend over and kiss them. That were ten years ago."

"What happened to the roses?" Mary asked, excited. "Did they die, too?"

"Wait 'til the spring," Ben said. "Wait 'til the sun shines and the warm rain gets to them, then tha'll see what happens." He stopped suddenly and looked at her eager face. "Why does tha care so much about roses?" he asked.

"I want to have a garden of my own," she told him.

As Mary skipped on through the gardens, she heard a whistling sound. She stopped. A boy was sitting under a tree, playing a wooden pipe. He was about twelve and

his cheeks were as red as poppies, his eyes the bluest Mary had ever seen. Two rabbits were sitting at his feet. Mary stood still until he stopped playing.

"I'm Dickon," he said at last, "and I know tha's Miss Mary. I've brought a little spade and tha seeds. Where's tha going to plant them?"

Mary's thin hands clutched each other. She did not know what to say. She went red, then white. "I don't know anything about boys," she said slowly. "Could you keep a secret if I told you one? It's a big secret. I don't know what I should do if anyone found out. I believe I should die!"

Dickon looked puzzled. "Aye," he said, "I can keep secrets."

Mary clutched his sleeve. "I've stolen a garden," she said very fast. "Nobody wants it, nobody cares for it, nobody ever goes into it." She burst into tears.

"Where is it?" Dickon whispered.

Mary led him to the door, took out the key and unlocked it. Dickon looked around him in silence. "I never thought I'd see this place," he whispered at last.

"So you know about it?" Mary asked in surprise.

"Aye," he said. "Martha told me."

"Will there be roses?" Mary asked.

"Dickon stepped over to one of the branches and scratched it with his knife.

"There's plenty of new bits," he told her, "the brown-green bits."

They went from tree to tree, from bush to bush as Dickon cut the dead wood away. Then he came to one of the little clearings where the bulbs grew.

"Who tidied this up?" he asked in surprise.

"I did," Mary said.

"Tha's done a lot of work for such a little thing," Dickon laughed.

"I'm growing fatter," Mary said, "and I'm growing stronger. I used to be tired, but when I dig, I'm not tired at all."

"There's still a lot of work to do here!" Dickon said.

"Will you come and help me?" Mary begged. "Please, Dickon!"

"I'll come every day if tha wants me, rain or shine," he told her.

Mary felt that however many years she lived she would never forget that first morning when her garden began to grow. Kneeling by Dickon as they planted the seeds, Mary stopped frowning and looked at him.

"Dickon," she said, "you are as nice as Martha said you were. You're the fifth person I like. Martha, your mother, Ben Weatherstaff and… the robin."

Dickon laughed out loud. "Tha's the strangest lass I ever saw!" he said.

CHAPTER FIVE

Cousin Colin

After her midday meal, Mary was rushing back into the garden when Martha stopped her.

"I've got something to tell you," she said. "Your uncle came back this morning and I think he wants to see you before he goes away again."

Mary turned pale. "When do you think he will want to see…?" she began.

As she spoke, the door opened and Mrs Medlock walked in. She was wearing her best black dress and cap.

"Go and brush your hair!" she said to Mary. "Martha, help her to put on her best dress. Mr Craven wants to see her in his study."

Mary's heart began to thump and she felt herself changing into a plain, silent child again. "My uncle won't like me," she thought, "and I shall not like him."

Mrs Medlock took her to a part of the house she had never seen before, into a room where a man was sitting by the fire.

"This is Miss Mary, sir," Mrs Medlock said.

She left Mary alone with Mr Craven. Mary stood there waiting, twisting her thin hands together.

"Come here!" her uncle said.

Mary went to him. He was not ugly. His face would have been handsome if he had not looked so unhappy.

"You are very thin," he said.

"I am getting fatter," Mary replied.

"I meant to send you a nurse or governess," he said, "but I forgot."

"Please… " Mary began, "I am… I am too big for a nurse, and please don't make me have a governess yet. I want to play out of doors. It makes me feel strong."

"You may do what you like, then," her uncle said kindly. "Don't look so frightened. I wish you to be happy, even if I am too unhappy to give you time or attention. Is there anything you want? Toys? Books? Dolls?"

"Can I have a bit of garden?" Mary asked. "To plant seeds in – to make things grow."

"You remind me of someone else who loved the earth and things that grow," he said softly. "You can have as much as you need."

"May I take it from anywhere?" Mary asked.

"Anywhere," he answered. "You must go now. I am tired! Goodbye. I shall be away all summer."

That night, the sound of rain woke Mary up. Suddenly another noise made her sit up. She listened.

"It isn't the wind now," she said in a loud whisper. "It is the crying I heard before. I must find out what it is."

Mary took the candle from the side of her bed and

went out into the corridor. The far-off, faint crying led her on, until she came to a door with a glimmer of light showing under it. Someone was crying in that room. Mary pushed open the door and went in.

In the four-poster bed sat a boy. He had a sharp and delicate face the colour of ivory. His eyes seemed too big for it. He had thick hair tumbling over his forehead. Mary crept across the room.

"Who are you?" the boy asked in a half-frightened whisper. "Are you a ghost?"

"No," Mary whispered. "Are you?"

"No," he said. "I am Colin. Colin Craven."

"I am Mary Lennox. Mr Craven is my uncle."

"He is my father," the boy said.

"Your father!" Mary gasped. "Why did nobody ever tell me? Did they tell you about me? We're cousins!"

Colin shook his head. "It would have frightened me," he said. "I won't let people see me."

"Why not?" Mary asked in surprise.

"I am always ill and my father thinks I may be a hunchback like him. But I shan't live that long!" Colin explained. "My father hardly ever comes to see me. My mother died when I was born and the sight of me makes him sad. He almost hates me."

"He hates the garden because she died," Mary said, half-speaking to herself.

"What garden?" Colin asked.

"The garden Mr Craven hates," she said nervously. "He locked the door. No one – no one knew where he buried the key. Do you want to live?" she said, trying to change the subject.

"No!" he answered crossly, "but I don't want to die. Talk about the garden again. I want to go there. I shall make them take me."

Mary's hands clutched each other. Why had she spoken about the garden out aloud? Everything would be spoiled now – everything. Dickon would never come back. And the garden would never be their secret again. "Oh, don't do that!" she cried. "If you make them take you in it will never be a secret again."

Colin leaned forward. "A secret," he said, "what do you mean?"

Mary words tumbled over one another. "You see, if no one knows but us – if there was a hidden door, if we could find it – if the garden was a secret and we could get into it, don't you see how much nicer it would be?"

Colin leaned back on his pillow.

"I could push you in your chair, and we could go alone, and it would be our secret garden," she went on.

"I would like that," said Colin, very slowly.

And Mary began to feel safer, because the idea of keeping the secret seemed to please him.

CHAPTER SIX

The quarrel

The moor was hidden in mist when morning came, and it was still raining.

"Martha, I have found out what the crying was," Mary said. "I heard it in the night. It was Colin. I found him."

Martha's face turned red with fright. "Oh, Miss Mary!" she cried, "tha'll get me into trouble!"

"He wants me to go and talk to him every day," Mary said. "And you are to tell me when he wants to see me."

"Me!" Martha cried again. "No! I shall lose my job!"

"You can't if you are doing what he wants," Mary said. "You all have orders to obey him. I think he is a very spoiled boy."

"He's been ill a lot," Martha said, "and now he's weak. His father fears he'll grow into a hunchback like him, but there's no sign of it."

Mary sat and stared into the fire. "I wonder," she said slowly, "if it would do him good to go out into a garden and watch things grow. It did me good."

"We once took him outside to see the roses," Martha answered. "Then he read somewhere that roses can make you sneeze. Well, he cried himself into a fever an' was ill all night."

Very soon afterwards, a bell rang and Martha had to go up to Colin. She came back ten minutes later, her face puzzled. "He's out of bed!" she told Mary, "and sitting in a chair reading. He wants you to go and talk to him."

Mary and Colin talked for a long time about everything – Dickon and the moor and India. They enjoyed themselves so much that they forgot about the time. They were laughing loudly over Ben Weatherstaff and his robin when the door opened and in walked Mrs Medlock and the doctor.

"What is going on?" the doctor asked crossly.

"This is my cousin, Mary Lennox," Colin said boldly. "I asked her to come and talk to me. She must come and talk to me whenever I send for her. She heard me crying in the night and found me. Nobody is to blame."

"Too much excitement is bad for you, my boy," the doctor said.

"I am better," Colin replied. "She makes me better."

On the first morning when the sky was blue again, Mary woke up very early. The moor was no longer brown and the birds were singing. Mary put her hand out of the window and held it in the sun.

"It's warm!" she cried. "It will make the green shoots grow! I can't wait. I'm going to see the garden now."

Mary put on her clothes in five minutes and left the house through a small side door. When she reached the door of the garden, a loud noise frightened her. She looked up at the top of the wall. There sat a huge glossy black bird. It flew into the garden with her and sat on a small apple-tree. And underneath the tree was a small, reddish animal with a bushy tail. Dickon was kneeling next to the animal, clearing the garden.

"This is my little fox cub," he explained, "and this giant bird is a crow."

"Oh Dickon!" Mary cried, "I'm so happy I can hardly breathe!"

They ran from one part of the garden to another, trying not to shout out too loud. The robin flew across the wall with pieces of straw for his nest.

"Dickon," Mary asked, "what do you know about Colin?"

"Mrs Medlock always stops at our cottage when she goes shopping in Thwaite," he said, "an' she tells us all about 'im. She knows she can trust us."

Mary told him about her midnight visit. "Do you think he wants to die?" she asked.

"No," Dickon replied, "but he wishes he'd never been born. His poor mother had a swing on that big tree over there. The branch broke and she fell. His eyes are so like hers that Mr Craven can't bear to look at 'im."

"He keeps thinking he can feel a lump coming on his back," Mary said.

"What if we could get 'im out 'ere," Dickon said. "No lad could get well if 'e lies in bed thinking about death."

The afternoon was busier than the morning. Dickon and Mary cleared nearly all the weeds from the garden and finished pruning most of the roses and trees. The sun was beginning to set when they left. Martha sighed as she came in.

"Master Colin's been in a tantrum all day," she said. "And watching the clock."

Colin was in bed when Mary went up to his room. "Why didn't you come to see me?" he demanded.

"I was working in the garden with Dickon," Mary replied.

"I won't let that boy come here if you stay with him so long," Colin said angrily.

"If you send Dickon away, I'll never come to see you again," Mary shouted.

"I'll make you!" Colin said loudly.

They glared at each other.

"You are a selfish thing!" Colin cried.

"You're more selfish than I am!" Mary answered.

"No, I'm not," he said, "because I'm always ill, and there's a lump coming on my back. I'm going to die!"

"You just say that to make people feel sorry for you," Mary cried. And she left the room.

In the middle of the night, a terrible noise woke her

up. It was Colin, screaming and crying. Mary ran along the corridor to his room.

"Stop it!" she shouted at him. "I hate you! Everybody hates you! I wish everybody would let you scream yourself to death. If you scream again, I'll scream, too, and I can scream louder than you!"

Colin was so surprised that he stopped screaming.

"I felt the lump – I felt it," he sobbed.

She peered down at his poor thin back. "There's not a single lump there," she said, "except backbone lumps. You can feel them because you're so thin."

"Have... have you found the way into the secret garden yet?" Colin asked, trying not to cry again.

Mary looked at his poor tired face, and felt sorry for him. "Yes, I think I have," she said.

"Oh, Mary!" Colin said, "if I could go into it, I think I should live long enough to grow up. Tell me what it looks like and I shall sleep."

"The roses have climbed and climbed," Mary began, "until they hang from the branches of the trees and they are creeping over the ground like a grey mist. The ground is full of daffodils and snowdrops and lilies and crocuses. The leaves are beginning to uncurl and green is showing everywhere. All the birds are coming to look at it because it is safe and still."

And Colin slept.

CHAPTER SEVEN

"I shall live for ever and ever!"

Mary slept late the next morning because she was tired. When she went out to the garden, she found that Dickon had come on his pony – and he had brought two tame squirrels. The fox and crow had followed him, too!

"He can tame any animal and any bird," Mary told Colin that evening.

"Mary," Colin said, "I want to see Dickon."

"I'm glad you said that!" Mary cried, "because... because... "

"Because what?" he asked eagerly.

Mary caught hold of both his hands. "Can I trust you?" she asked. "I trusted Dickon because birds and animals trust him. Can I trust you for sure?"

"Yes – yes!" Colin cried.

"Well," Mary went on, "Dickon will come to see you tomorrow morning and he'll bring his creatures with him." She paused with excitement. "But that's not all," she said. "The rest is better. I've found the door to the garden."

"Shall I live to see it?" Colin gasped.

"Of course you will!" Mary snapped impatiently. "Don't be silly!"

Colin began to laugh at himself. Mary sat on a stool next to him and talked about the garden.

"It sounds as if you really have seen it," Colin said.

Mary hesitated for a moment. At last, she boldly told the truth. "I have," she said, "I found the key and got in weeks ago. I didn't dare tell you before. I wasn't sure I could trust you."

"You can," he smiled.

When Dickon came to see Colin the next day, he was carrying a newborn lamb and the little red fox trotted by his side. The crow and the squirrels peeped from his pockets. Colin had never talked to a boy in his life and he did not know what to say. But Dickon was not in the least shy or awkward. He gave the lamb to Colin with a feeding bottle. Then they looked at pictures in a gardening book of all the plants in the secret garden.

"I'm going to see them!" Colin cried.

"Aye, tha mun," Mary laughed, trying out her Yorkshire.

One fine afternoon, a few days later, the strongest man in the house carried Colin downstairs and put him in his wheelchair. Dickon was waiting outside to push the chair. Mary walked beside it. Colin leaned back and lifted his face to the sky where small snowy clouds floated like white birds. The wind blew softly from the moor. At last, they came to the ivy-covered walls.

"This is it," Mary whispered.

"I shall not look until I am inside," Colin said, covering his eyes.

Mary opened the door and Dickon pushed him in with one strong, steady splendid push. Colin took his hands away from his eyes and looked round. A veil of fair green leaves hung everywhere, and here and there were splashes of gold and purple and white.

The sun fell warm upon Colin's face. "I shall get well!" he cried. "Mary! Dickon! I shall get well! And I shall live for ever and ever and ever!"

CHAPTER EIGHT
Walking tall

Mary and Dickon worked here and there in the garden while Colin watched them. Every moment of his afternoon was filled with new things and the sunshine became more golden.

"I wonder if we shall see the robin," Colin said.

"Aye," Dickon replied, his voice low and gentle. "Tha'll see 'im soon when the eggs hatches out. Tha'll see 'im flying backwards and forwards catching worms."

"That big tree over there, it's dead, isn't it?" Colin asked.

"Aye," Dickon said. "But the roses are climbing over it. It won't look dead then. It'll be the prettiest of them all."

"It looks as if the big branch has broken off," Colin said. "I wonder how it was done."

"Look, there's the robin!" Dickon said, breathing a sigh of relief.

"It was the magic that sent the robin just then," Mary whispered, "and stopped Colin finding out how his mother died."

They stayed in the garden until the sun turned to gold.

"I don't want this afternoon to end," Colin sighed, "but I shall come back tomorrow. I'm going to see everything grow here. I'm going to grow here myself."

"Tha'll be diggin' and walkin' like us," Dickon said.

Colin's face flushed. "Walk!" he said. "Dig! Shall I?"

Dickon did not know what to say. Neither he nor Mary had ever asked if there was anything wrong with Colin's legs.

"There's nothing actually wrong with them," Colin said at last. "They're just thin and weak and they shake when I try to stand up. I... "

Suddenly, he stopped speaking and pointed to the garden wall.

"Who's that man?" he asked.

"What man?" Mary and Dickon cried together.

They turned round. There, standing on the top rung of a ladder, was Ben Weatherstaff. He shook his fist at Mary.

"Tha's a bad lass!" he shouted, "pokin' tha nose in."

"It was the robin that showed me the way!" she shouted back angrily.

Ben Weatherstaff suddenly caught sight of Colin. He stopped shaking his fist and his mouth dropped open.

"Do you know who I am?" Colin asked. "Do you? Answer!"

"Aye, I do," the old man answered at last. "Tha

mother's eyes staring at me! But tha's a cripple!"

Colin's face turned scarlet and he sat bolt upright.

"I'm not! I'm not!" he shouted furiously.

Colin's anger and pride made him forget everything and filled him with a power he had never known before.

"Come here, Dickon!" he cried, pulling the blanket from his legs.

Dickon held Colin's arm as his thin feet touched the grass. Then Colin stood upright, as tall and as straight as an arrow.

"Look at me! Look!" he cried.

"He's as straight as any lad in Yorkshire!" Dickon said.

Tears ran down Ben Weatherstaff's wrinkled cheeks. Colin looked him straight in the face.

"I'm your master when my father is away," he said. "This is my garden. Don't dare say a word to anybody about it. Now take down your ladder and come in through the door."

"Yes, sir!" the old man whispered.

When he had gone, Colin pointed to a nearby tree.

"I'm going to walk over there," he said. "I'm going to be standing when Weatherstaff comes in."

"You can do it! You can do it!" Mary muttered under her breath.

Colin did walk to the tree and was very steady, although Dickon still held his arm.

"Do I look like a cripple?" Colin asked as soon as Ben Weatherstaff came through the garden door.

The gardener shook his head.

"This was my mother's garden, wasn't it?" Colin asked him.

"Aye, it was!" he replied.

"It's my garden now and I shall come here every day," Colin said. "But it is to be a secret. I shall send for you sometimes to help – but you must come when no one can see you."

Ben Weatherstaff's face twisted itself into a dry old smile.

"I've come 'ere before when no one saw me," he said

quietly. "She was such a pretty young thing, tha mother. I promised I'd take care of the roses. I came until two years ago, when I was too old to climb in over the wall."

"I'm glad you did, Weatherstaff," Colin smiled. "Now I know you can keep a secret!"

Colin looked down at Mary's trowel on the grass. He leaned over and picked it up. An odd expression came to his face as he started to dig the earth with it.

"You can do it! Mary whispered to herself. "I tell you, you can!"

"I shall fetch a rose for you to plant, sir," Ben Weatherstaff said.

While he was gone, Dickon dug the hole wider and Mary fetched water.

"I want to do it before the sun goes down," Colin whispered.

Ben Weatherstaff brought the rose in its pot from the greenhouse and handed it to Colin. Colin's thin white hand shook a little as he placed it in the hole.

"It's planted!" he said at last. "And the sun is slipping down. Help me up, Dickon. I want to be standing when it goes. That's part of the magic."

And Dickon helped him and the magic gave him strength. As the sun slipped below the horizon and ended that strange, lovely afternoon, Colin stood on his two feet – laughing.

CHAPTER NINE
Magic!

Amazing things happened in the months that followed. The seeds Dickon and Mary had planted grew and their stalks danced in the breeze. The roses grew out of the grass, tangling in the tree-trunks, hanging from the branches, spreading everywhere. They came alive day by day, hour by hour. The buds were tiny at first. Then they began to swell until they burst open, filling the air with their scent.

"It's magic!" Mary said.

"Even if it isn't real magic, we can pretend it is," Colin said. "The sun is shining – that is magic," he chanted. "The flowers are growing – that is magic. Being alive is magic. The magic is in me and in all of us."

Mary listened to him in amazement. Then, suddenly, Colin stopped.

"Now I am going to walk around the garden," he announced. And he did. "The magic is in me!" he kept saying. "It is making me strong! I can feel it!"

He looked at them all. "Nobody is to know anything about it until I am strong," he cried, "especially the doctor. And when my father comes back home, I shall just walk into his study."

There was one problem – and Dickon found himself telling his mother all about it when he went home. "Master Colin's so hungry all the time," he explained. "He's supposed to be ill so he can't ask for any more food. Miss Mary's hungry, too, being out in the fresh air all day."

Dickon's mother laughed at first, then she looked serious. "I know a way to help them, lad," she said. "Take a pail of milk when tha goes in the morning. And I'll bake a crusty loaf for them."

Colin was right to be worried. The doctor was suspicious. "You are getting fatter," he said, "and your colour is better. Your father will be happy to hear of this improvement."

"You mustn't tell him!" Colin shouted angrily. "It will only disappoint him if I get worse again. You are making me angry and that is bad for me. I feel hot already!"

"Sssh, my boy," the doctor said. "I shall do nothing without your permission."

And so the play-acting went on. Every morning, Dickon brought fresh milk and bread and freshly baked currant buns.

"Magic is in Dickon's mother just as it is in him!" Colin said.

Her kindness led to other kindnesses. Colin and Mary realised that Dickon's mother now had two extra mouths to feed. They sent some money to her and some extra to buy eggs and potatoes. And every beautiful morning, the magic worked and Colin grew stronger.

"The boy is a new creature," the doctor said to Mrs Medlock.

"So is the girl," she replied. "She's begun to be pretty now that she's filled out. Her hair's grown thick and healthy looking and she's got colour in her cheeks. She and Master Colin laugh together like a pair of crazy people. Perhaps they're growing fat on that."

"Perhaps," the doctor agreed. "Let them laugh."

CHAPTER TEN
In the garden

One morning, out in the garden, Colin threw his trowel on to the ground. He stretched himself to his full height and threw out his arms. His face glowed with colour.

"Mary! Dickon!" he cried. "Just look at me!"

They stopped their weeding and stared at him.

"I'm well!" he cried. "I've wished for it all this time. But now I feel well. I shall never stop making magic."

Suddenly, he looked worried. "There is somebody coming!" he whispered.

A woman had pushed open the garden door. "It's mother!" Dickon cried.

Mrs Sowerby flushed with pleasure when she saw Colin. "Are you surprised that I am so well?" Colin asked her. Mrs Sowerby put her hand on his shoulder and smiled tearfully. "Aye, I am," she said, "but my heart jumped just then because tha's so like thy mother."

"Do you think that will make my father like me?" Colin asked her.

"Aye, dear lad," she whispered. "He mun come home now. He mun come home."

While the secret garden was coming alive and two children were coming alive with it, Mr Craven was travelling across Europe, as he had done for the last ten years. His mind was always full of unhappy thoughts. At night, he dreamed about his dead wife and her garden.

One day, Mr Craven received a letter arrived from England. He did not recognise the handwriting on the envelope and he tore it open quickly.

"Dear Sir," he read,

"Please, Sir, I would come home if I was you. I think you would be glad to come – if you will excuse me, sir – I think your wife would ask you to come if she was here,

Your obedient servant,

Susan Sowerby (Martha's mother)"

Mr Craven set off at once for Yorkshire, afraid that his son was now very ill, or even dying. Thoughts of his wife, and her garden, swirled around his head.

"I will try to find the key," he thought, "I will try to open the door. I must – though I don't know why."

As soon as Mr Craven arrived at Misselthwaite Manor, he sent for Mrs Medlock. "How is Master Colin?" he asked her.

"He's… he's different, sir," she answered. "He insists on being taken into the garden every day with Miss Mary and Susan Sowerby's boy, Dickon."

"How does he look?" Mr Craven asked.

"He laughs all the time when he's with Miss Mary," Mrs Medlock said. "He never used to laugh at all."

"Where is Master Colin now?" Mr Craven asked.

"In the garden, sir," she told him.

"In the garden!" he said, after he had sent Mrs Medlock away. "In the garden."

Mr Craven set off slowly to the hidden door. He stopped outside the garden. Where had he buried that key ten long years ago? Then he jumped in surprise. He could hear sounds coming from the other side of the wall. Somebody was running and laughing in there. "Race you to the door!" a voice cried. Was he hearing things? The feet inside seemed to run faster, the shouts grew louder and the door in the wall burst open.

A boy ran through it at full speed, straight into him. Mr Craven put out his hands to stop the boy falling. He stared in amazement. The boy in front of him was tall and glowing with life. He pushed the thick hair back from his forehead and lifted a pair of grey eyes – eyes rimmed with thick black lashes. It was the eyes that made Mr Craven gasp. "Who... what... who?" he asked.

This was not what Colin had planned. But perhaps this was even better. "Father," he said, "I'm Colin."

"In the garden! In the garden!" his father whispered.

"Yes," Colin said, "it was the garden that did it, and Mary and Dickon – and the magic. No one knows. We kept it a secret until you came home." He touched his father's arm. "Aren't you glad, father?" he asked.

Mr Craven put his hands on his son's shoulders and held him still. He dared not speak for a while. "Take me into the garden, my boy," he said at last.

Colin led his father through the door. The secret garden was full of autumn colour, purple, violet and flaming scarlet. The sun deepened the yellowing leaves to gold. Mr Craven looked round. "I thought it would be dead," he said at last.

They sat down under a tree – all except Colin, who wanted to stand while he told the story.

A little later Mrs Medlock glanced out of a window and shrieked in surprise, "Come and look at this!" All the servants came running to see. Across the lawn came the master of Misselthwaite – and by his side, head held high and eyes full of laughter, walked Master Colin!